# Get pupils' knowledge in order with CGP!

Looking for a simple way to help pupils learn all the key facts and methods for Year 4 Maths?  Well, look no further — this Knowledge Organiser is the perfect solution!

We've condensed each topic down to the essentials, so it covers exactly what pupils need, with clear diagrams and tables.

And that's not all!  There's a matching Year 4 Maths Knowledge Retriever — a great way of making sure pupils have got to grips with the content of every page.

# CGP – still the best!  ☺

Our sole aim here at CGP is to produce the highest quality books — carefully written, immaculately presented and dangerously close to being funny.

Then we work our socks off to get them out to you — at the cheapest possible prices.

Published by CGP

Editors: Sarah George, Ruth Greenhalgh, Rachel Hickman, Hannah Lawson,
    Sean McParland, Ali Palin, Sarah Pattison and Dave Ryan.

With thanks to Gareth Mitchell and Glenn Rogers for the proofreading.

With thanks to Jan Greenway for the copyright research.

ISBN: 978 1 78908 868 7

Printed by Elanders Ltd, Newcastle upon Tyne.
Clipart from Corel®

Based on the classic CGP style created by Richard Parsons.

# Contents

# Place Value

## Place Value

The value of a digit depends on its place in the number.

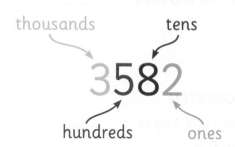

thousands

tens

**3582**

hundreds

ones

This number is three thousand, five hundred and eighty-two.

10 ones = 1 ten

10 tens = 1 hundred

10 hundreds = 1 thousand

| Th | H | T | O |
|----|---|---|---|
|    | 10| 0 | 0 |

| Th | H | T | O |
|----|---|---|---|
| 1  | 0 | 0 | 0 |

## Partitioning

**Partitioning** is breaking up numbers into smaller, easier parts.

You can partition using place value:

**9241**

9000     200     40     1

9241 is made up of 9 thousands, 2 hundreds, 4 tens and 1 one.

9241 = 9000 + 200 + 40 + 1

## Roman Numerals

Roman numerals are letters that stand for numbers.

These are the first few:

I = 1    V = 5     X = 10

L = 50   C = 100

**1** More than one of the same numeral in a row — add together.

XX = 10 + 10 = 20

**2** Smaller numeral before a bigger one — subtract.

IV = 5 − 1 = 4

**3** Smaller numeral after a bigger one — add.

LV = 50 + 5 = 55

## Ordering and Comparing

To order whole numbers:

**1** Count the number of digits — numbers with more digits are bigger.

**2** If numbers are the same length, compare them digit by digit, from left to right.

< means "is less than"

> means "is greater than"

Or you can partition in other ways:

9241 = 9200 + 40 + 1

9241 = 9100 + 121 + 20

9241 = 9011 + 230

**4** Convert numbers in stages.

XCIV

XC = 100 − 10 = 90      IV = 5 − 1 = 4

90 + 4 = 94

**EXAMPLE**

Put these numbers in order from smallest to biggest: 1280, 964, 1137, 1246

964 has the fewest digits,

so it's the smallest.

The other numbers all have 1 thousand, so compare the hundreds:

964, 1137, 1280, 1246

Then compare the tens:

964, 1137, 1246, 1280

So the order is: 964, 1137, 1246, 1280.

## Decimals

Decimals show numbers that aren't whole. They have a decimal point. Digits after the decimal point are worth less than 1.

ones          hundredths

3.19

decimal point          tenths

You say "three point one nine".

3.19 is between 3 and 4.

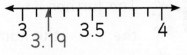

3  3.19  3.5  4

# Counting On

## Finding 1000 More or Less

To find 1000 more than a number, add 1 to the thousands digit.

Find 1000 more than 673.

673 has 0 thousands, so the answer has 0 + 1 = 1 thousand.

673 + 1000 = 1673

To find 1000 less than a number, subtract 1 from the thousands digit.

What is 3302 − 1000?

3302 has 3 thousands,

so the answer has 3 − 1 = 2 thousands.

3302 − 1000 = 2302

## Counting in 6s, 7s and 9s

You can count in 6s, 7s or 9s using number lines.

To count in 6s, start at zero and take 6 steps at a time.

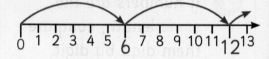

You get 6, 12, 18, 24, and so on.  These numbers are the 6 times table.

They're called multiples of 6.

Negative numbers have a minus sign in front of them.

## Counting with Negative Numbers

Negative numbers are numbers that are less than zero.

Numbers left of zero are negative.          Numbers right of zero are positive.

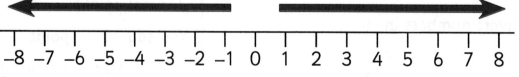

The further left, the lower the number.

The further right, the higher the number.

You can also use **times tables** to count in multiples:

6, 12, 18, 24, 30, 36, 42, 48, 54, 60, 66, 72

7, 14, 21, 28, 35, 42, 49, 56, 63, 70, 77, 84

9, 18, 27, 36, 45, 54, 63, 72, 81, 90, 99, 108

EXAMPLE

Xi's party is in exactly 4 weeks. How many days is this?

You need to find 4 lots of 7, so count on four 7s from 0.

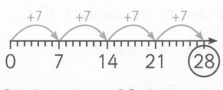

So 4 weeks is 28 days.

## Counting in 25s and 1000s

Counting in multiples of 25:
In every 100, there are four lots of 25.
Between each hundred,
there is a 25, a 50 and a 75.

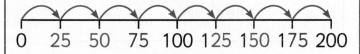

0  25  50  75  100  125  150  175  200

**EXAMPLE**

A box weighs 7000 g. A bag weighing 2000 g is put inside it. How much do they weigh together?

Count on two 1000s from 7000:

7000, 8000, 9000

Together they weigh 9000 g.

To count in multiples of 1000, add 1 to the thousands digit each time. The last 3 digits are always 000:

1000, 2000, 3000, 4000, 5000

**EXAMPLE**

Use a number line to work out 3 − 7.

Start at 3.
Count back 7 places.

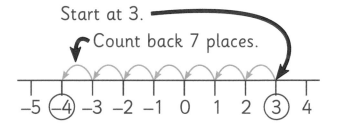

So 3 − 7 = −4.

−5 −4 −3 −2 −1 0 1 2 3 4

# Rounding and Estimating

## Rounding to the Nearest 10, 100 or 1000

You can round numbers using a **number line**.

1. Find the multiples of 10, 100 or 1000 on either side of the number.

2. Sketch a number line. Mark on your number and the two possible answers.

3. Round to the closer answer.

> If your number is halfway between the two possible answers, round up.

**EXAMPLE**

What is 47 rounded to the nearest 10?

47 has 4 tens, so is between 40 and 50.

40        ↑47        50

47 is closer to 50 than to 40, so round up to 50.

## Rounding Decimals

To round a decimal to the nearest whole number:

1. Find the two whole numbers the decimal is between.

2. Look at the digit to the right of the decimal point — the decider.

3. If it's less than 5, round down. If it's 5 or more, round up.

**EXAMPLE**

El is 1.2 m tall. Round her height to the nearest metre.

1.2 is between 1 and 2.

The decider is 2.    1.2

2 is less than 5, so round down to 1 m.

You can also round numbers using this method:

**1** Find the two possible answers, one on either side of the number.

**2** Look at the digit to the right of the place being rounded to — the decider.

**3** If the decider is less than 5, then round down.
If the decider is 5 or more, then round up.

Round 3086 to the nearest 100.

3086 is between 3000 and 3100.

The decider is 8.  3086

8 is more than 5, so round up to 3100.

## Estimating Numbers

You can estimate numbers between points on a scale.

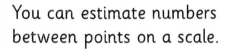

30                50

The arrow is near the middle of 30 and 50.  It could be pointing to 40.

Estimate the temperature shown on this thermometer.

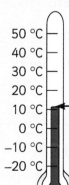

The temperature is between 10 °C and 20 °C, but it is much closer to 10 °C.

It is approximately 11 °C or 12 °C.

You can give measurements to the nearest whole unit, or nearest ten, etc.

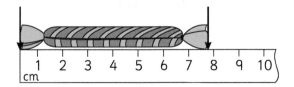

This sweet is between 7 cm and 8 cm long.  It is closer to 8 cm, so it measures 8 cm to the nearest centimetre.

# Addition and Subtraction

## Written Addition

Arrange the numbers in place value columns.

Start adding from the column with the smallest place value.

### EXAMPLE

What is 6245 + 2174?

**①** Add the ones.

```
 Th H  T  O
    6  2  4  5
 +  2  1  7  4
             9
```
Line up the ones.

**②** Add the tens.

```
 Th H  T  O
    6  2  4  5
 +  2  1  7  4
          1  9
       1
```

4 + 7 = 11, so put 1 in the tens column and carry 1 to the hundreds column.

**③** Add the hundreds.

```
 Th H  T  O
    6  2  4  5
 +  2  1  7  4
       4  1  9
       1
```

Add the carried digit:
2 + 1 + 1 = 4

## Estimating and Checking

Compare your answer to an estimate to check it.

**1** Round each number, e.g. to the nearest ten.

**2** Work out the calculation with the rounded numbers.

To check 57 + 91 = 148:

57 is about 60 and 91 is about 90, so 57 + 91 is about 60 + 90 = 150.

150 is close to 148, so this is sensible.

Or check it using inverse operations.

Adding and subtracting are inverses.

Inverse means 'opposite'.

To check 42 − 17 = 15:

The inverse of '−17' is '+17'.

15 + 17 = 32, not 42,

so this answer is wrong.

## Written Subtraction

**4** Add the thousands.

```
   Th H  T  O
      6  2  4  5
   +  2  1  7  4
      8  4  1  9
         1
```

6245 + 2174 = 8419

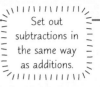
Set out subtractions in the same way as additions.

**EXAMPLE**

Work out 7853 – 3689.

**1** Subtract the ones.

```
   Th H  T   O
      7  8  ⁴5̶ ¹3
   -  3  6  8   9
                4
```

You can't do 3 – 9, so exchange 1 ten for 10 ones: 13 – 9 = 4

**2** Subtract the tens.

```
   Th H   T   O
      7 ⁷8̶ ¹⁴5̶ ¹3
   -  3  6  8   9
               6  4
```

You can't do 4 – 8, so exchange 1 hundred for 10 tens: 14 – 8 = 6

**3** Subtract the hundreds, then the thousands.

```
   Th H   T   O
      7 ⁷8̶ ¹⁴5̶ ¹3
   -  3  6  8   9
      4  1  6   4
```

So 7853 – 3689 = 4164

## Addition and Subtraction Problems

**EXAMPLE**

Hattie buys a magnet for £1.54 and a key ring for £1.63. She pays with a £5 note. How much change does she get?

You need to exchange across two columns.

**1.** Add the amounts together.

```
   O  t  h
   1 . 5  4
 + 1 . 6  3
   3 . 1  7
   1
```

Line up the decimal points.

**2.** Subtract the total from £5.

```
     O    t   h
   ⁴5̶ . ⁹0̶¹ ¹0
   - 3 .  1   7
     1 .  8   3
```

She gets £1.83 change.

# Using Times Tables

## The 6, 7 and 9 Times Tables

### 6 times table
1 × 6 = 6
2 × 6 = 12
3 × 6 = 18
4 × 6 = 24
5 × 6 = 30
6 × 6 = 36
7 × 6 = 42
8 × 6 = 48
9 × 6 = 54
10 × 6 = 60
11 × 6 = 66
12 × 6 = 72

### 7 times table
1 × 7 = 7
2 × 7 = 14
3 × 7 = 21
4 × 7 = 28
5 × 7 = 35
6 × 7 = 42
7 × 7 = 49
8 × 7 = 56
9 × 7 = 63
10 × 7 = 70
11 × 7 = 77
12 × 7 = 84

### 9 times table
1 × 9 = 9          7 × 9 = 63
2 × 9 = 18         8 × 9 = 72
3 × 9 = 27         9 × 9 = 81
4 × 9 = 36        10 × 9 = 90
5 × 9 = 45        11 × 9 = 99
6 × 9 = 54        12 × 9 = 108

## Factor Pairs

Factors of a number: whole numbers that divide exactly into the number.

Factor pair: two factors of a number that multiply together to make the number.

## The 11 and 12 Times Tables

### 11 times table
1 × 11 = 11        7 × 11 = 77
2 × 11 = 22        8 × 11 = 88
3 × 11 = 33        9 × 11 = 99
4 × 11 = 44       10 × 11 = 110
5 × 11 = 55       11 × 11 = 121
6 × 11 = 66       12 × 11 = 132

### 12 times table
1 × 12 = 12        7 × 12 = 84
2 × 12 = 24        8 × 12 = 96
3 × 12 = 36        9 × 12 = 108
4 × 12 = 48       10 × 12 = 120
5 × 12 = 60       11 × 12 = 132
6 × 12 = 72       12 × 12 = 144

## Mental Multiplying and Dividing

To multiply three numbers together, work it out in steps.

**EXAMPLE**

Work out $5 \times 2 \times 9$.

**1.** Multiply two numbers: $5 \times 2 = 10$

**2.** Multiply the result by the third number: $10 \times 9 = 90$

A number multiplied or divided by 1 doesn't change. A number multiplied by O is O.

Multiplying and dividing are inverses, so you can use times tables to help you divide.

To work out $84 \div 12$, look at the 12 times table:

$7 \times 12 = 84$,

so $84 \div 12 = 7$

Use easy calculations to help you solve harder ones.

**EXAMPLE**

What is $560 \div 7$?

$56 \div 7 = 8$. 560 is 10 times bigger than 56, so $560 \div 7 = 8 \times 10 = 80$.

**EXAMPLE**

Find all the factor pairs of 18.

**❶** Starting with 1, work out what to times each number by to make 18.

| | |
|---|---|
| $1 \times 18 = 18$ | $4 \times ? = \times$ |
| $2 \times 9 = 18$ | $5 \times ? = \times$ |
| $3 \times 6 = 18$ | $6 \times 3 = 18$ |

**❷** You can't make factor pairs from 4 or 5, so they aren't factors of 18.

**❸** Keep going until you repeat a pair. $6 \times 3$ is the same as $3 \times 6$, so stop.

So the factor pairs of 18 are: 1 and 18, 2 and 9, and 3 and 6.

You can multiply in any order:

3

4

$3 \times 4 = 12$        $4 \times 3 = 12$

3 lots of 4        4 lots of 3

# Multiplication and Division

## Written Multiplication

**1** Line up the place value columns.

**2** Multiply the one-digit number by each part of the big number, starting from the column with the smallest place value.

**3** Carry digits to the next column if needed.

## Written Division

1 Divide the hundreds, tens and ones in the big number by the small number, in turn.

2 Write the result of each division on top, in the same place value column.

3 If the division isn't exact, exchange with the next column.

In written division, start with the biggest place value. When you add, subtract or multiply, start with the smallest.

**EXAMPLE**

What is 875 ÷ 7?

```
      1
  7 | 8 ¹7 5
```

$8 \div 7 = 1$ with 1 left over.
Put a 1 on top, and exchange
1 hundred for 10 tens.

```
      1 2
  7 | 8 ¹7 ³5
```

$17 \div 7 = 2$ with 3 left over.
Put a 2 on top, and
exchange 3 tens for 30 ones.

```
      2 7 3
  ×       6
      3 8
    4   1
```

70 × 6 = 420, then add the carried ten: 420 + 10 = 430.

Put 3 in the tens column and carry 4 to the **hundreds** column.

```
      2 7 3
  ×       6
  1 6 3 8
      4   1
```

200 × 6 = 1200, then add the carried 4 hundreds: 1200 + 400 = 1600.

Put 6 in the **hundreds** column and carry 1 to the thousands column.

So 273 × 6 = 1638

## Multiplication and Division Problems

**EXAMPLE**

Asif makes 9 piles of pebbles. Each pile has 17 pebbles.
How many pebbles are there in total?

He has 9 lots of 17 pebbles.
17 = 10 + 7, so 9 × 17 = 9 × 10 + 9 × 7.
9 × 10 = 90 and 9 × 7 = 63. 90 + 63 = 153, so there are 153 pebbles in total.

**EXAMPLE**

Paula equally shares a box of 27 sweets between 4 people. How many sweets are left over?
The biggest multiple of 4 that is less than 27 is 6 × 4 = 24.
27 − 24 = 3, so there will be 3 sweets left over.

```
      1 2 5
  7 | 8 7 ¹5 ³5
```

35 ÷ 7 = 5. Put a 5 on top.
There's nothing left to exchange, so 875 ÷ 7 = 125.

# Fractions

## Fraction Basics

Fractions show numbers that aren't whole.

**Numerator** (top number): shows how many parts you have.

$$\frac{7}{8}$$

**Denominator** (bottom number): shows how many equal parts something has been divided into.

## Equivalent Fractions

**Equivalent fractions** are equal but written differently.

## Hundredths

This square is divided into one hundred equal parts. Each part is 1 hundredth of the square.

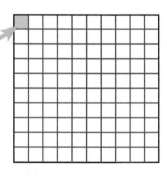

$$1 \text{ hundredth} = \frac{1}{100}$$

$$100 \text{ hundredths} = 1 \text{ whole}$$

This rectangle is divided into ten equal parts. Each part is 1 tenth.

$$1 \text{ tenth} = \frac{1}{10}$$

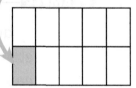

Dividing each tenth by ten gives one hundred equal parts. Each part is 1 hundredth.

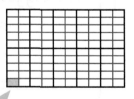

## Counting in Hundredths

To count up in hundredths, add 1 to the numerator each time.

To count down, subtract 1 from the numerator.

The denominator is always 100.

Equivalent fractions take up the same amount of a shape.

3 out of 6 parts
are shaded.

$\frac{3}{6}$ of the shape
is shaded.

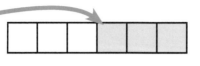

1 out of 2 parts
is shaded.

$\frac{1}{2}$ of the shape
is shaded.

The same amount of each shape is shaded, so $\frac{3}{6}$ is equivalent to $\frac{1}{2}$.

**EXAMPLE**

Use the diagram
below to show that
$\frac{3}{12}$ is equivalent to $\frac{1}{4}$.

**1** Group the shaded
parts together.

**2** Draw a circle to show $\frac{1}{4}$.
Split it into 4 equal parts
and shade 1 part.

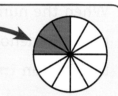

**3** The circles have the same amount
shaded, so $\frac{3}{12} = \frac{1}{4}$.

**EXAMPLE**

Count up in hundredths from $\frac{19}{100}$. Stop after three steps.

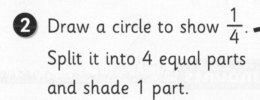

+1     +1     +1

$\frac{19}{100}$    $\frac{20}{100}$    $\frac{21}{100}$    $\frac{22}{100}$

# Fraction Calculations

## Adding and Subtracting Fractions

When fractions have the same denominator, add or subtract the numerators.

Leave the denominators as they are.

**EXAMPLE**

Work out $\dfrac{15}{23} - \dfrac{6}{23}$.

Subtract the numerators:

$$\dfrac{15}{23} - \dfrac{6}{23} = \dfrac{15 - 6}{23} = \dfrac{9}{23}$$

The answer to fraction calculations can be bigger than 1.

When the numerator is bigger than the denominator, the fraction is called an **improper fraction**.

**EXAMPLE**

What is $\dfrac{8}{10} + \dfrac{3}{10}$?

Add the numerators:

$$\dfrac{8}{10} + \dfrac{3}{10} = \dfrac{8 + 3}{10} = \dfrac{11}{10}$$

## Fractions of Amounts

To find a fraction of an amount, **multiply** by the **numerator** (top number) and **divide** by the **denominator** (bottom number).

*You can divide first, then multiply, if that's easier.*

**EXAMPLE**

Find $\dfrac{2}{3}$ of 12.

$\dfrac{2}{3}$

Multiply by the numerator:
$12 \times 2 = 24$

Divide by the denominator:
$24 \div 3 = 8$

So $\dfrac{2}{3}$ of 12 = 8

**EXAMPLE**

Work out $\dfrac{7}{12}$ of 48 cm.

Divide by the denominator:
$48 \div 12 = 4$

Multiply by the numerator:
$4 \times 7 = 28$

So $\dfrac{7}{12}$ of 48 cm = 28 cm

You can write improper fractions as **mixed numbers**, with a whole number part and a fraction part.

$$\frac{11}{10} = \frac{10}{10} + \frac{1}{10}$$

$$= 1 \text{ whole} + \frac{1}{10}$$

$$= 1\frac{1}{10}$$

You can check answers to fraction calculations by drawing diagrams.

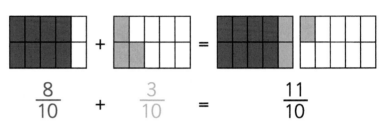

$$\frac{8}{10} \quad + \quad \frac{3}{10} \quad = \quad \frac{11}{10}$$

## Fraction Problems

1. Pick out the key information.

2. Write it as number sentences.

3. Do one step at a time.

**EXAMPLE**

A jug contains $\frac{7}{8}$ of a litre of water.

$\frac{4}{8}$ of a litre is poured out.

How much water is left in the jug?

To work out $\frac{7}{8} - \frac{4}{8}$, subtract the numerators:

$$\frac{7}{8} - \frac{4}{8} = \frac{7-4}{8} = \frac{3}{8}$$

So $\frac{3}{8}$ of a litre of water is left.

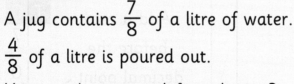

**EXAMPLE**

Al had £24.
He lost five twelfths of it.
How much money does Al have left?

Find $\frac{5}{12}$ of £24:

£24 ÷ 12 = £2

£2 × 5 = £10

Then subtract from £24:

£24 − £10 = £14

Fractions and Decimals    17

# Decimals

## Decimal Basics

Decimals show numbers that aren't whole.

2 tens

9 ones

1 tenth

8 hundredths

decimal point

$$29.18$$

Digits after the decimal point are worth less than 1.

## Comparing Decimals

To compare decimals, look at the digits in each place. If the digits in one place are the same, compare digits in the next place to the right.

## Fractions and Decimals

You can write fractions showing tenths and hundredths as decimals.

$$\frac{1}{10} = 1 \text{ tenth} = 0.1$$

$$\frac{1}{100} = 1 \text{ hundredth} = 0.01$$

Write the number of tenths or hundredths in the correct place.

$$\frac{3}{10} = 3 \text{ tenths} = 0.3$$

$$\frac{6}{100} = 6 \text{ hundredths} = 0.06$$

$$\frac{48}{100} = 48 \text{ hundredths}$$

$$= 40 \text{ hundredths} + 8 \text{ hundredths}$$

$$= 4 \text{ tenths} + 8 \text{ hundredths} = 0.48$$

10 hundredths = 1 tenth

## Dividing by 10 and 100

To divide by 10, move each digit 1 place to the right.

The number gets 10 times smaller.

$$80 \div 10 = 8$$

| T | O | . | t |
|---|---|---|---|
| 8 | 0 | . |   |
|   | 8 | . |   |

You don't need a zero here.

$$7 \div 10 = 0.7$$

| T | O | . | t |
|---|---|---|---|
|   | 7 | . |   |
|   | 0 | . | 7 |

Add a zero before the decimal point.

Learn these fraction to decimal conversions:

$$\frac{1}{4} = 0.25 \qquad \frac{3}{4} = 0.75$$

$$\frac{1}{2} = 0.5$$

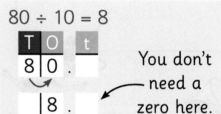

**Ascending**: from smallest to biggest.
**Descending**: from biggest to smallest.

To divide by 100, move each digit 2 places **to the** right.

The number gets 100 times smaller.

$20 \div 100 = 0.2$

| T | O | . | t |
|---|---|---|---|
| 2 | 0 | . |   |
|   | 0 | . | 2 |

**Add a zero before the decimal point.**

$3 \div 100 = 0.03$

| T | O | . | t | h |
|---|---|---|---|---|
|   | 3 | . |   |   |
|   | 0 | . | 0 | 3 |

**Add a zero between the decimal point and the first digit.**

**EXAMPLE**

Put these in ascending order:
4.66, 3.21, 4.59, 4.63

**1** Compare and order the ones:
3.21, 4.66, 4.59, 4.63

**2** Then the tenths:
3.21, 4.59, 4.66, 4.63

**3** Then the hundredths:
3.21, 4.59, 4.63, 4.66

**4** Ascending order is:
3.21, 4.59, 4.63, 4.66

## Decimal Problems

Read the question carefully, and work it out one step at a time.

**EXAMPLE**

Mia found 0.75 kg of rubbish, Ahmed found 0.72 kg and Si found $\frac{76}{100}$ kg. Who found the most rubbish?

Mia: 0.75 kg          Ahmed: 0.72 kg          Si: $\frac{76}{100}$ kg = 0.76 kg

Each amount has 0 ones and 7 tenths, so compare the hundredths.

6 is bigger than 5 or 2, so 0.76 is the biggest number.

So Si found the most rubbish.

# Units and Time

## Converting Units

1 km = 1000 m          1 litre = 1000 ml          1 kg = 1000 g

### EXAMPLE

Ayesha walked 2.6 km.
How far is this in metres?

2.6 km = 2.6 × 1000
       = 2600 m

### EXAMPLE

Krish used 0.3 litres of paint.
How much is this in ml?

0.3 litres = 0.3 × 1000
           = 300 ml

## Comparing Measurements

Convert measurements to the same
units before you compare them.

### EXAMPLE

A baker uses 1.6 kg of sugar
and 1475 g of butter.
Which does she use more of?

1 Convert the amount
  of sugar to grams:

  1.6 kg = 1.6 × 1000
         = 1600 g

2 Then compare:

  1600 g is greater than 1475 g,
  so she uses more sugar.

## Money

There are 100 pence (p)
in a pound (£).

Amounts of money can be
written using two decimal
places, e.g.

£3.56 means £3 and 56p

£9.02 means £9 and 2p

£4.00 means £4

### EXAMPLE

A pack of cheese costs £2.57.
A loaf of bread costs 94p.
How much more does
the cheese cost
than the bread?

## 12- and 24-Hour Clocks

You can show time on an analogue, 12-hour or 24-hour clock:

Times in the 12-hour clock use 'am' or 'pm' to show morning or afternoon/evening.

For times in the afternoon and evening:

+ add 12 to the hours to go from the 12-hour to the 24-hour clock
− subtract 12 to go from the 24-hour to the 12-hour clock.

**EXAMPLE**

What is twenty past nine in the evening in the 24-hour clock?

Twenty past nine in the evening is 9:20 pm in the 12-hour clock.

9 + 12 = 21, so this is 21:20 in the 24-hour clock.

## Units of Time

1 minute = 60 seconds

1 hour = 60 minutes

1 year = 12 months

1 week = 7 days

Write 94p as a decimal, then subtract:

94p = £0.94

$$\begin{array}{r} \overset{1}{\cancel{2}}.\overset{1}{5}7 \\ -0.94 \\ \hline 1.63 \end{array}$$

So the cheese costs £1.63 more.

**EXAMPLE**

Jason watched a film that lasted 2 hours and 17 minutes. How long was the film in minutes?

1 hour = 60 minutes

So 2 hours = 2 × 60

= 120 minutes

So the film lasted

120 + 17 = 137 minutes

# Perimeter and Area

**Perimeter**: the distance all the way around the outside of a 2D shape.

To find the perimeter, add up the lengths of all the sides of the shape.

### EXAMPLE

Find the perimeter of this shape.

Mark where you start with a cross, then go all the way round the shape until you get back to the cross.

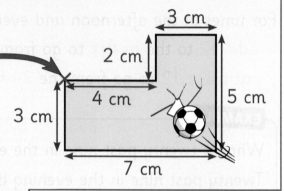

Perimeter = 4 cm + 2 cm + 3 cm

+ 5 cm + 7 cm + 3 cm

= 24 cm

### EXAMPLE

What is the area of this shape?

There are 6 squares, so the area is 6 cm².

## Areas

1. To find the area of a shape drawn on a grid, count the number of squares it covers.

2. Make sure you add up any half-squares too. Remember, two halves make a whole.

### EXAMPLE

Find the area of the shape below.

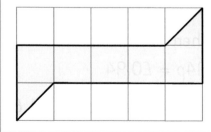

You can find the perimeter of a square or rectangle using the properties of the shape, even if some side lengths are missing.

**EXAMPLE**

What is the perimeter of this square?

All sides of a square are equal,
so every side is 5 cm long.

So the perimeter is 5 cm + 5 cm + 5 cm + 5 cm = 20 cm

5 cm

You could also
do 4 × 5 cm
= 20 cm

**EXAMPLE**

What is the perimeter of this football pitch?

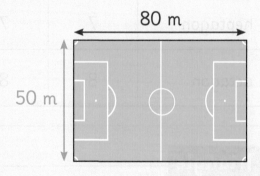

80 m

50 m

Opposite sides of a rectangle are equal,
so the missing vertical side is 50 m
and the missing horizontal side is 80 m.

So the perimeter is:
50 m + 80 m + 50 m + 80 m
= 260 m

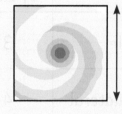

Each square in these
grids is 1 cm².

The shape covers
5 whole squares
and 2 half-squares.

Area = $5 + \frac{1}{2} + \frac{1}{2}$

      = 6 cm²

# Shapes and Angles

## Polygons

Polygons are 2D shapes with straight sides.

| Polygon | Number of sides | Number of angles |
|---|---|---|
| triangle | 3 | 3 |
| quadrilateral | 4 | 4 |
| pentagon | 5 | 5 |
| hexagon | 6 | 6 |
| heptagon | 7 | 7 |
| octagon | 8 | 8 |

## Quadrilaterals

Quadrilaterals are polygons with 4 sides.

**Kite**

2 pairs of equal sides

No parallel sides

## Angles

A whole turn is 360°.

Angles are measured in degrees (°).

A $\frac{1}{4}$ turn is 90°.

## Types of Triangle

**Equilateral**

Each angle is 60°.

3 equal sides
3 equal angles

**Isosceles**

2 equal sides
2 equal angles

**Right-angled**

1 right angle

## Square

4 right angles

4 equal sides

2 pairs of parallel sides

## Rectangle

4 right angles

2 pairs of equal sides

2 pairs of parallel sides

## Rhombus

4 equal sides

Opposite angles are equal

Opposite sides are parallel

## Parallelogram

2 pairs of equal sides

Opposite angles are equal

Opposite sides are parallel

## Trapezium

1 pair of parallel sides

A square is used to show a right angle.

A $\frac{1}{4}$ turn is a **right** angle.

An angle that is less than a $\frac{1}{4}$ turn is an **acute** angle.

An angle that is bigger than a $\frac{1}{4}$ turn but less than a $\frac{1}{2}$ turn is an **obtuse** angle.

## EXAMPLE

Put angles A-C in order of size, from smallest to largest.

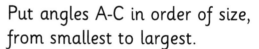

B is less than a $\frac{1}{4}$ turn, so it is an acute angle.

C is a $\frac{1}{4}$ turn, so it is a right angle.

A is more than a $\frac{1}{4}$ turn, so it is an obtuse angle.

So the order is B, C, A.

## Scalene

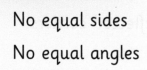

No equal sides

No equal angles

# Symmetry Symmetry

## Lines of Symmetry

A mirror line that can be drawn through a shape is called a line of symmetry. When a mirror is placed on this line, it looks as if you can see the whole shape.

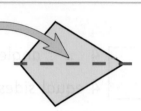

A shape can have more than one line of symmetry:

    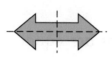  

no lines of symmetry      1 line of symmetry      2 lines of symmetry      3 lines of symmetry

## Drawing Symmetrical Shapes

To reflect a shape in a mirror line:

1. Choose one corner of the shape and count the number of squares between the corner and the mirror line.

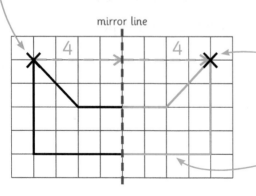

## Completing Patterns

You can use lines of symmetry to make symmetrical patterns.

2. Count the same number of squares on the other side of the mirror line and draw the reflected corner at that point.

3. Repeat for the rest of the corners.

4. Join up the reflected corners with straight lines.

## Finding Lines of Symmetry

To find lines of symmetry:

**1** Look for places where a line would split the shape in half.

**2** Then check if the two halves are mirror images of each other:

> Put a mirror on the line and check if you can see the whole shape.

OR

> Fold along the line and check if all the edges line up.

These lines all split the shape in half, and the halves are mirror images of each other.
This shape has 4 lines of symmetry.

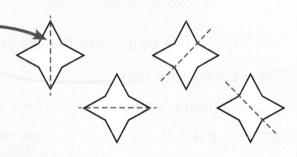

**EXAMPLE**

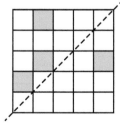

Colour in 4 more squares to make this pattern symmetrical in the mirror line.

The colouring has to be the same on both sides of the mirror line.

You need to colour in 3 squares below the mirror line.

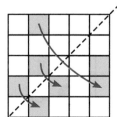

Then colour in 1 square above the mirror line.

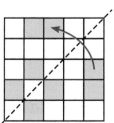

# Coordinates and Translations

## Coordinates

Coordinates are two numbers that tell you the position of a point on a grid.
You find them by using the x-axis and the y-axis.

The y-axis is a vertical line that goes up the left side of the grid.

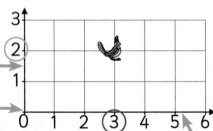

The x-axis is a horizontal line across the bottom of the grid.

(0, 0) is called the origin.

The bird's coordinates are: (3, 2)

Coordinates are always written in brackets.

The x-coordinate tells you how many units across a point is.

The y-coordinate tells you how many units up a point is.

## Translations

A translation is where a shape slides from one place to another.
The shape stays the same, and it doesn't rotate or flip over.

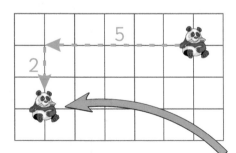

The panda has been translated
5 squares left and 2 squares down.

To describe a translation:

1 Pick a corner of the shape.

2 Count how many squares it's moved left or right.

3 Count how many squares it's moved up or down.

To help to remember the order of coordinates:

- x comes before y in the alphabet.

- You always go in a house (→), before you go up (↑) the stairs.

**EXAMPLE**

What are the coordinates of point A?

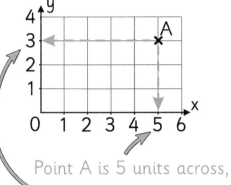

Point A is 5 units across,

and 3 units up.

So the coordinates are (5, 3).

## Joining Points

Plot points and then join them with straight lines to make a polygon.

**EXAMPLE**

Plot these points on the graph:

(1, 2)   (3, 7)   (6, 7)   (6, 4)

What shape do they make when joined together?

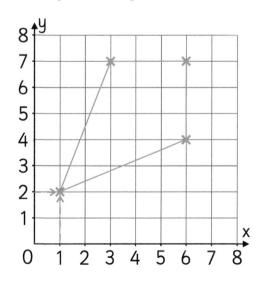

The shape is a kite.

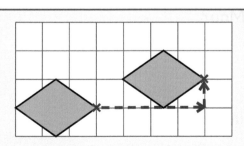

This shape has been translated 4 squares right and 1 square up.

# Tables, Charts and Graphs

## Tables

Data can be displayed in a **table**.

**EXAMPLE**

How many more arms does Zob have compared to Zip?

|       | Zob | Bev | Zip |
|-------|-----|-----|-----|
| Arms  | 5   | 2   | 3   |
| Eyes  | 2   | 4   | 1   |

Zob has 5 arms.

Zip has 3 arms.

So Zob has 5 − 3 = 2 more arms.

## Bar Charts

The heights of the bars on a **bar chart** show how many things are in each category.

This chart shows people's votes for their favourite zoo animal:

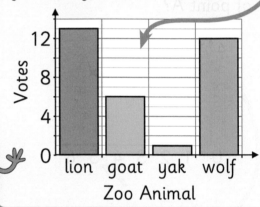

## Pictograms

**Pictograms** use pictures to represent data.

A key tells you how many items each picture represents.

**EXAMPLE**

This pictogram shows how many books Prisha read over three months. How many books did she read in April and May?

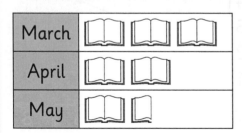

Key: 📖 = 2 books

In April, she read 2 × 2 = 4 books.

A full picture means 2 books, so half a picture means 1 book.

In May, she read 2 + 1 = 3 books.

So she read 4 + 3 = 7 books.

The bar for the lion is the tallest, so it got the most votes.

The bar for the yak is the shortest, so it got the least votes.

A **time graph** shows how something changes over time.

The graph below shows the temperature change of water in a glass.

The temperature after 6 minutes was 30 °C. To plot this point:

**1** Find the time on the horizontal axis and go up.

**2** Find the other value on the vertical axis and go across.

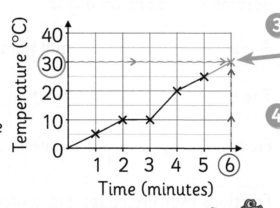

**3** Draw a cross where the two lines meet.

**4** Join the points with a straight line.

**EXAMPLE**

The graph on the right shows how far Steve was from his home during a walk. How much further away was he after 7 hours than after 2 hours?

Read up from the horizontal axis.

After 7 hours he was 10 km away.

After 2 hours he was 3 km away.
So after 7 hours he was
10 – 3 = 7 km further away.

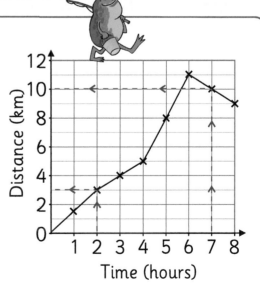

# Glossary

| | |
|---|---|
| **Acute angle** | An angle that is less than a right angle (90°). |
| **Area** | The space inside a 2D shape. |
| **Ascending** | From the smallest to the biggest. |
| **Bar chart** | A chart where the heights of the bars show how many things are in that category. |
| **Coordinates** | Two numbers that tell you the position of a point on a grid. |
| **Decimal** | A number that has a decimal point and isn't whole. |
| **Denominator** | The bottom number on a fraction. |
| **Descending** | From the biggest to the smallest. |
| **Equivalent fractions** | Fractions that are equal, but written differently. |
| **Factor** | A whole number that divides exactly into a number. |
| **Factor pair** | Two factors of a number that multiply together to make the number. |
| **Fraction** | A way of showing part of a whole. |
| **Improper fraction** | A fraction where the numerator is bigger than the denominator. |
| **Inverse** | The opposite calculation. |

| | |
|---|---|
| **Key** | Something that tells you how many items each picture represents on a pictogram. |
| **Line of symmetry** | A mirror line that can be drawn through a shape. |
| **Mixed number** | A number with a whole number part and a fraction part. |
| **Negative number** | A number that is less than zero. |
| **Numerator** | The top number on a fraction. |
| **Obtuse angle** | An angle that is bigger than a right angle (90°) but less than 2 right angles (180°). |
| **Partitioning** | Breaking up numbers into smaller, easier parts. |
| **Perimeter** | The distance around the outside of a 2D shape. |
| **Pictogram** | A graph that uses pictures to represent data. |
| **Polygon** | A 2D shape with straight sides. |
| **Quadrilateral** | A polygon with four sides. |
| **Roman numeral** | A letter that stands for a number. |
| **Table** | A way of showing data using rows and columns. |
| **Time graph** | A graph that shows how something changes over time. |
| **Translation** | When a shape slides from one place to another. |

# Index